INTRODUCTION

Welcome to sailing! I am thrilled to be able to guide you through your first steps into such an amazing and enjoyable sport.

Sailing is truly a sport for all, offering something for everyone, regardless of age and ability. The RYA scheme has been designed to help you progress easily and accessibly.

The RYA National Sailing Scheme is run at RYA Training Centres around the UK and overseas, all of which have been independently inspected to create a safe and enjoyable learning environment.

RYA Start Sailing is designed as an accompaniment to the RYA Start Sailing Level 1 and Basic Skills Level 2 courses as well as a reference tool assisting you with your first times afloat. Each chapter will guide you through essential information on areas key to learning the sport, including rigging, launching, and turning the boat.

Enjoy your time afloat!

Amanda Van Santen

RYA Chief Instructor,
Dinghy & Windsurfing

NOTE:
Words in red have their definitions in the Glossary on pages 72–75.

Where can you Sail?

The world is rich in places to sail. You will find sailing clubs, centres and boating facilities on many lakes, reservoirs and rivers, as well as superb coastal sailing areas. You can also take a course during a holiday at an RYA Recognised Training Centre overseas.

The RYA National Sailing Scheme

The RYA National Sailing Scheme is taught in dinghies, keelboats, and multihulls.

Dinghies

Learning in a dinghy is a great way to start sailing. Dinghies used for teaching are stable and simple to sail, but still rewarding and challenging.

Starting in a single-handed dinghy can be the quickest way to learn but, on the other hand, you may enjoy learning with others in a larger boat designed to be sailed by two or more people. The choice is yours!

Keelboats

A keelboat is slightly larger than a dinghy and has a weighted keel under the hull which prevents it capsizing, so it tends to be more stable and dry.

Multihulls

Most multihulls have two hulls.

The combination of stability and light weight means that multihulls are very fast and offer exhilarating sailing. Most multihulls are designed to be sailed by two people but there are several types that are sailed single-handed. Multihulls require slightly different sailing techniques compared to boats with a single hull. Although multihulls and trimarans (boats with three hulls) are very stable they can still capsize if allowed to heel (lean over) too far.

1. CLOTHING & PERSONAL EQUIPMENT

Buoyancy Aid

Spray Top

Fingerless Gloves

Short Wetsuit (Summer)

Wetsuit Shoe

Spray Top

Three-quarter-length Wetsuit (Spring/Autumn)

Boot

Buoyancy Aid

Full-fingered Gloves

Winter Wetsuit

Drysuit

Staying Comfortable

There is no need to be cold and wet when you are sailing. Modern sailing clothing is warm and comfortable, providing good freedom of movement. Pick your clothing to suit when and where you sail. Even in the summer you can get colder on the water than ashore, and the temperature is likely to fluctuate more. Staying warm is usually associated with staying dry, and most types of outer-layer sailing clothing aim to keep water away from the inner layers and your skin. Sailing a dinghy generally means you will get wet, so wearing a wetsuit will insulate your body, complemented by a spray top and trousers. In the winter, thermal or fleece clothing can be used for inner layers.

Picking the Right Clothing

When you start learning, your clothing, such as a wetsuit, spray top and trousers, will often be provided by your sailing school. When buying your own gear, take into consideration when and where you sail. Good waterproofs plus thermal inner layers are suitable for stable dinghies or keelboats, but think about using a wetsuit for faster dinghies or multihulls, especially in the winter. Wetsuits are usually made from neoprene and provide some insulation by trapping a thin layer of water between the body and the suit. The water is then warmed up by body heat. A summer suit has short arms and legs and is designed for hot conditions. It is generally 2mm in thickness. A spring/autumn suit has short arms and three-quarter or full-length legs. It is generally 3mm thick. A winter suit is designed for cold conditions and covers the full body. It is 5mm thick.

Once you improve your skills and start to sail fast boats, a drysuit which uses neck, ankle and wrist seals keeps all water out, meaning you are warm and dry. However, overheating can also be a problem so pick your clothing to suit the conditions.

Wetsuit shoes and boots are made from neoprene and rubber, and provide you with some insulation and grip. For sailing, boots can be more robust than general wetsuit shoes.

Personal Safety Gear

Personal safety gear is essential. A buoyancy aid is designed to help you stay afloat should you capsize. It is usually the most appropriate choice for dinghy or multihull sailing. An inflatable lifejacket may be an alternative for keelboat sailors only.

TOP TIP

Most heat loss occurs through the top of the head, so wear a warm hat when sailing in cold weather.

2. PARTS OF THE BOAT

Understanding the Language

You only need to know a few basic terms when you start to learn and it is sufficient to know the names for the parts of the boat shown here.

Two important words are port and starboard. The port side is the left side (looking forward) and always remains so, even if you turn round to face astern (backwards)!

The term windward means the side closest to the wind – the 'upwind' side of the boat.

Leeward is the downwind side of the boat.

Bow and stern refer to the front and back of the boat.

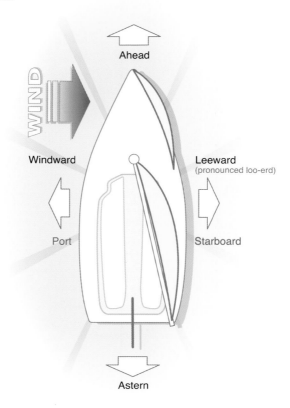

Sails and their Parts

The simplest boats use a single sail attached behind the mast. This is called the mainsail. Most boats have a mainsail plus another sail, the jib, which is in front of the mast. Both sails are controlled by ropes called sheets. The mainsail has a mainsheet attached to the boom which is used to adjust the angle of the boom to the boat. The jib has two jib sheets – one for each side of the boat.

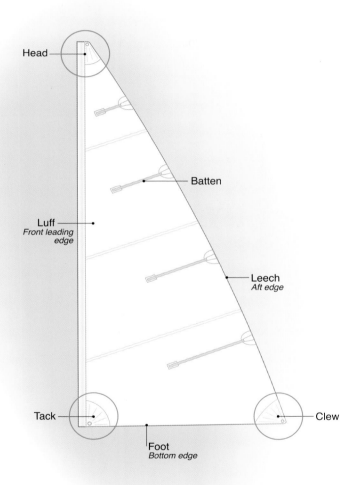

Head

Batten

Luff
Front leading edge

Leech
Aft edge

Tack

Foot
Bottom edge

Clew

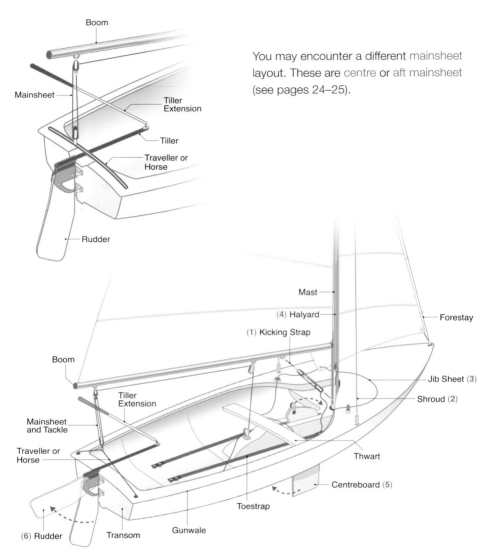

You may encounter a different mainsheet layout. These are centre or aft mainsheet (see pages 24–25).

Boom

Mainsheet

Tiller Extension

Tiller

Traveller or Horse

Rudder

Mast

(4) Halyard

(1) Kicking Strap

Forestay

Boom

Jib Sheet (3)

Tiller Extension

Shroud (2)

Mainsheet and Tackle

Traveller or Horse

Thwart

Centreboard (5)

Toestrap

(6) Rudder

Transom

Gunwale

The kicking strap (1) tackle holds the boom down when sailing.

Shrouds (2) hold the mast up and attach to the shroud plates.

The jib sheet (3) (rope) is led through a fairlead and held by a cam cleat.

The halyard (4) (rope) that hoists the sail is held by a clam cleat.

The centreboard (5) pivots up or down to act as a keel.

The rudder (6) attaches to the boat's transom and is removable.

3. TYPES OF BOAT

A Single-handed Dinghy

Single-handed dinghies are very popular because they are easy to transport, rig, launch and sail, letting you arrive at a venue and go sailing within minutes. They are also relatively low in cost and light in weight.

Most single-handed dinghies have a single sail (the mainsail) set on a simple mast that does not need shrouds to hold it upright. The sail usually has a simple sleeve at the luff which we call the 'luff sleeve'. The mast then slides into the sleeve and then goes into a socket in the deck.

The controls are equally simple. The mainsheet (**1**) controls the position of the sail, while the kicking strap (**2**) holds the boom down. There are toestraps (**3**) to tuck your feet under when sitting out, and a tiller extension (**4**) for steering.

Most single-handed dinghies have a daggerboard (**5**) which slides vertically through the bottom of the boat and prevents the boat from sliding sideways. Other types of dinghy may use a pivoting centreboard which does the same job.

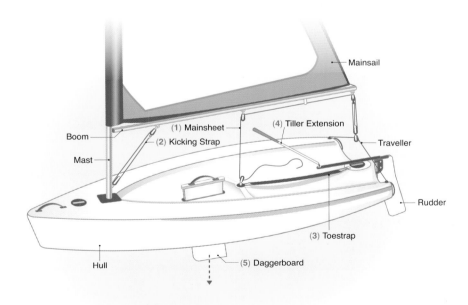

Try out a range of boats when you start sailing to find out which type you enjoy most. Many clubs and centres have boats available for hire.

Keelboats

Keelboats are not as common as dinghies but there is still a fair selection to choose from.

All the normal equipment you would find in a dinghy will be present, except for a centreboard or daggerboard. Instead, a weighted keel gives the boat its stability. In some keelboats, the keel can be raised to make it easier to store or transport the boat ashore.

As well as the normal controls there may also be some other gear, such as winches, that make it easier to set the sails on the larger boat.

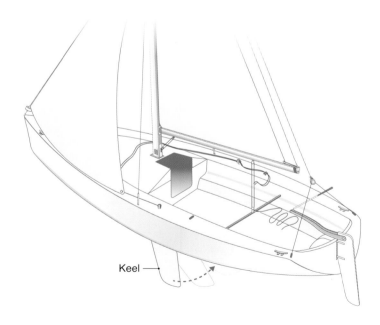

Keel

Multihulls

Multihulls have two hulls, which are connected by crossbeams. A fabric trampoline is laced to the two crossbeams and hulls, providing a large area for the crew. Many multihulls use a loose-footed mainsail, which means they don't have a boom. The mainsheet is attached directly to the clew of the sail and the mast partially rotates, which makes the mainsail more efficient.

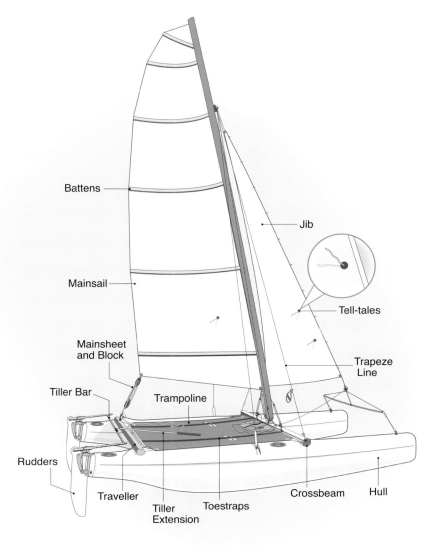

Battens

Jib

Mainsail

Tell-tales

Mainsheet and Block

Trapeze Line

Tiller Bar

Trampoline

Rudders

Traveller

Tiller Extension

Toestraps

Crossbeam

Hull

4. RIGGING YOUR BOAT

Preparing the Boat for Sailing

The process of attaching and hoisting sails is known as rigging the boat. For your first sail, an instructor or experienced sailor will show you how to attach the sails in readiness for hoisting them before you go afloat. The different types of dinghies, keelboats and multihulls all have their own ways of attaching and hoisting sails but the principles remain the same.

Trolleys

Most dinghies and multihulls have launching trolleys built to suit their shape. Always tie the bow of the boat to the trolley handle to prevent it sliding off, and make sure the boat is sitting correctly on the supports before moving it.

Take care when moving a boat on a trolley. Always look up to make sure the mast does not hit overhead obstructions such as power cables. Be careful not to lose control when going down a slipway! If the mainsail is hoisted, leave the kicking strap slack as this will depower the sail.

Hoisting Sails

It is generally easier to hoist sails ashore but this will depend on the wind direction and strength. The key points to remember are:

• Hoist the jib first.

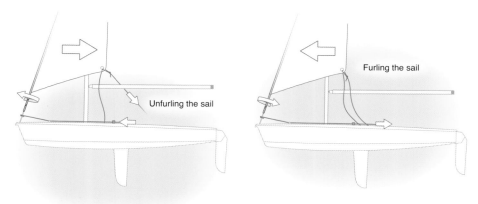

Unfurling the sail

Furling the sail

- Provided the sheets are loose, it will flap freely.
- The jib can usually be hoisted before launching.
- The mainsheet and the kicking strap must be completely slack before hoisting the mainsail.

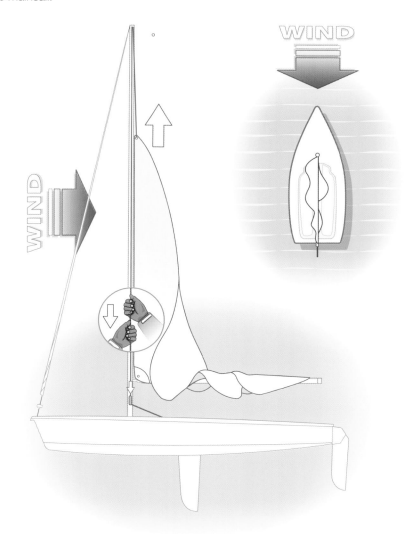

- Point the boat exactly into the wind before hoisting the mainsail so that it can flap freely.
- To make launching easier you may choose to hoist the mainsail once the boat is afloat.

Reducing Sail Area

In order to maintain control in strong winds it may be necessary to reduce the amount of sail you use. This is called reefing. Most single-handed dinghies can be reefed by rolling the sail around the mast. In two-person dinghies it can be reefed by rolling or flaking the mainsail around the boom.

Whatever method your boat uses, it is easier to reef ashore than afloat. If in doubt, put in a reef before you launch. You can always take the reef out afloat if you find you do not need it.

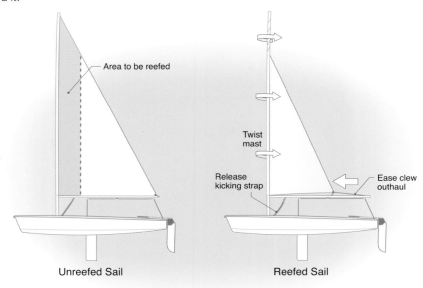

Unreefed Sail   Reefed Sail

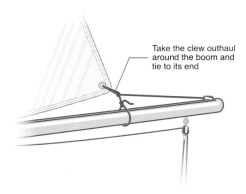

Take the clew outhaul around the boom and tie to its end

TOP TIP

Before hoisting the mainsail, turn the boat directly into the wind and release the kicking strap and mainsheet.

Launching the Boat

Wheel the boat on its trolley to the launching point, ensuring that all the bungs are in place sealing the boat, and attach the rudder and tiller. If your boat uses a daggerboard, make sure that it is in the boat and check that your buoyancy aid is secure.

Now you are ready to go!

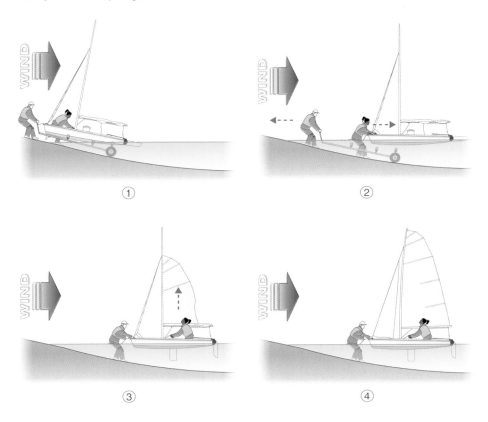

Wheel the boat into the water until it floats off its trolley, undoing the rope securing the boat to the trolley handle. With someone holding the boat by its bow, allow it to swing round to point into the wind. Pull the trolley clear of the water and park it out of the way of other slipway users.

Getting Away from the Shore

Your RYA Recognised Training Centre will have a safe open sailing area where you can learn your basic skills. Check the wind direction before you sail away – the jib is a useful indicator. Once sailing it is all too easy to focus inside the boat, so remember to keep a good lookout at all times.

Your instructor may tow you out to the sailing area or you might paddle or row away from the shore if a launching area is constricted or the wind is blowing directly onto the shore, making it difficult to sail off. In a single-handed dinghy you can sit on the tiller extension to steer while you paddle.

6. BASIC SKILLS

Steering

Once your boat is away from the shore in clear water you will be able to start steering under sail. The person who steers is called the helm, while the others on board are called the crew.

The helm generally sits on the windward side of the boat forward of the tiller and holds the tiller extension in his or her rear hand. In a two-person boat the crew sits just forward of the helmsman.

On your first sail you will learn how to steer the boat using the tiller extension. By pushing or pulling on the tiller extension, the rudder will turn to change the boat's course.

TOP TIP

You can only steer a car when it is moving – a boat is the same and if it slows down too much it will not respond to the tiller.

Points of Sailing

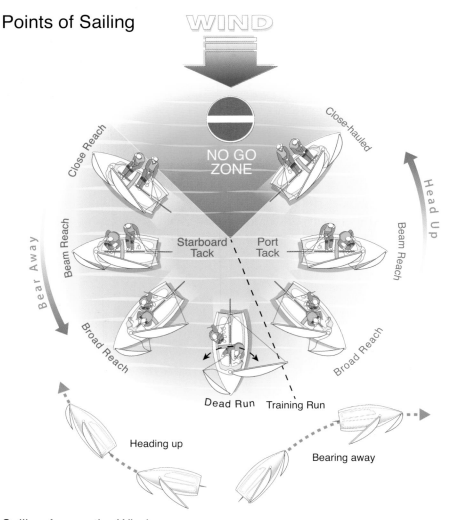

Sailing Across the Wind

One of the delights of sailing is that the boat is completely reliant on the wind. This means that you must be aware of the wind direction and also its strength.

On your first sail you will start by steering on a beam reach (across the wind) with the wind coming over the side of the boat. This is the easiest point of sailing on which to practise steering the boat.

You can sail in two directions on a beam reach – on port tack, when the wind comes over the port side, and on starboard tack, when the wind comes across the starboard side. On a beam reach the sails are set about halfway out, with the centreboard about halfway down.

Sailing Upwind

Turn towards the wind (luff) onto a close reach. Pull the sails in until they stop flapping. Put the centreboard three-quarters down. This helps resist the increased side force.

Turn further towards the wind and pull the sails in tight to sail close-hauled, putting the centreboard fully down. This is the closest angle a sailing boat can sail to the wind. If you sail any closer the sails will start flapping and the boat will slow down. This is when the heeling force is also at its greatest, so sit out on the windward side of the boat to keep the boat upright!

To sail directly upwind it is necessary to follow a zigzag course turning (tacking) through 90 degrees each time.

Sailing to Windward

To go upwind, sail as close to the wind as you can. Sailing close-hauled efficiently means sailing on the edge of the no-go zone without turning into it.

- The crew pulls the jib in tight and can cleat the sheet.
- The helmsman steers by watching the jib tell-tales.
- Luff gently until the windward tell-tales lift. Then, if the boat starts to slow down, bear away until both tell-tales stream together. If sailing a single-hander, use the tell-tales on the mainsail.

The No Go Zone

The area between the two close-hauled courses, on either side of the wind direction, is called the No Go Zone. If you sail too close to the wind into the No Go Zone the sail loses all power and you will slow down and stop. When you are sailing upwind you should always be aware of where the wind is coming from so that you stay on the edge of the No Go Zone. Having something to aim for (i.e. a new goal point for your close-hauled course) is very helpful, and the more you practise the quicker you will start to feel when you are getting too close to the wind.

Sailing Downwind

From a beam reach, turn away from the wind (bearing away) onto a broad reach. As you turn downwind let the sails out to keep them set at the correct angle to the wind, with the centreboard raised three-quarters.

- Move the crew inboard.
- Bear away more and, with the sails out and the jib falling slack in the wind shadow of the mainsail, the boat is now on a run with the mainsail right out.
- Pull the centreboard almost all the way up.
- Sailing on a run can be quite confusing when you start, so luff up until the jib fills again and sail on a training run. This is a more stable route downwind. Sit one on either side to balance the boat.

Tacking and Gybing

To change course from port to starboard tack (or vice versa) when sailing upwind, turn the bow through the wind. This is known as tacking. When sailing downwind, turn the stern through the wind. This is known as gybing. More information on both these techniques is covered later in the book.

Stopping and Starting

Sailing boats do not have brakes so to stop you have to make use of your boat controls and the wind. To do this, turn the boat onto a close reach and let out the sails until they flap. The boat will stop in the 'lying-to' position with the sails out on the leeward side. It is also possible to stop by turning head to wind, but the boat will not stay in this position for long. Use the lying-to position whenever you need to stop the boat temporarily. To start sailing again, pull in the sails and, as the boat moves forwards, steer onto the new course.

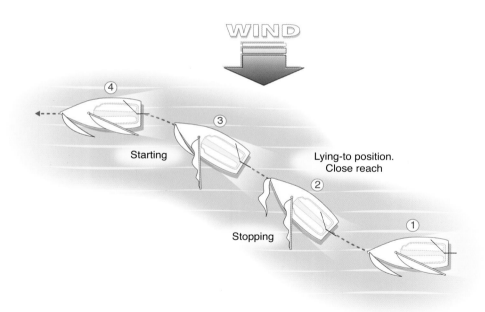

Steering the Boat

Although the rudder steers the boat, this is not the only control. It is important to adjust the sails and the crew and helm position to balance, and the centreboard as you turn. Practise turning the boat and making adjustments to the controls as you turn towards and away from the wind.

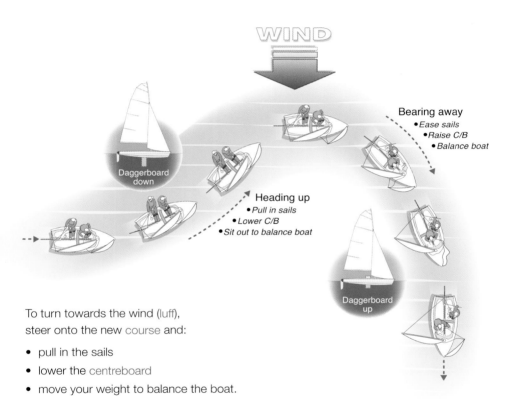

To turn towards the wind (luff), steer onto the new course and:

- pull in the sails
- lower the centreboard
- move your weight to balance the boat.

To turn away from the wind (bear away):

- steer onto the new course
- let out the sails
- raise the centreboard
- move your weight to balance the boat.

7. TACKING

Tacking involves turning the boat so that the bow passes through the wind while the sails and the crew change sides. Helm and crew need to work together to turn the boat, moving your weight to the new side and trimming the sails. The basic principles apply to all boats but different equipment may require different techniques.

The easiest way to learn is to tack from one beam reach to the other. To tack successfully, maintain speed before the tack and hold the tiller over until the turn is complete.

Tacking with a Centre Mainsheet

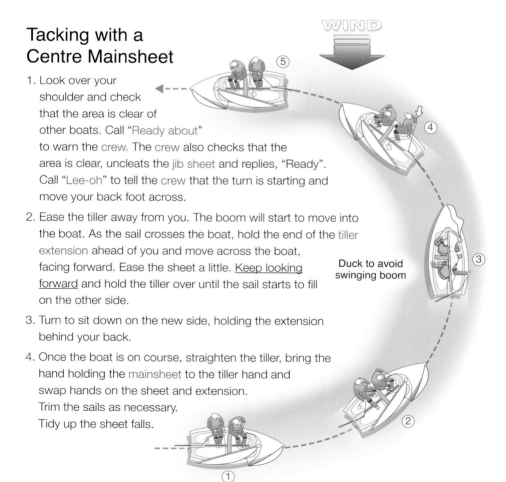

1. Look over your shoulder and check that the area is clear of other boats. Call "Ready about" to warn the crew. The crew also checks that the area is clear, uncleats the jib sheet and replies, "Ready". Call "Lee-oh" to tell the crew that the turn is starting and move your back foot across.

2. Ease the tiller away from you. The boom will start to move into the boat. As the sail crosses the boat, hold the end of the tiller extension ahead of you and move across the boat, facing forward. Ease the sheet a little. Keep looking forward and hold the tiller over until the sail starts to fill on the other side.

Duck to avoid swinging boom

3. Turn to sit down on the new side, holding the extension behind your back.

4. Once the boat is on course, straighten the tiller, bring the hand holding the mainsheet to the tiller hand and swap hands on the sheet and extension. Trim the sails as necessary. Tidy up the sheet falls.

Tacking with an Aft Mainsheet

Tacking a boat with an aft mainsheet is slightly different. Change hands on the mainsheet and tiller extension before the tack, and cross the boat facing the stern.

1. Look over your shoulder and check that the area is clear of other boats.

2. Call "Ready about", then change hands on the tiller extension and the mainsheet.

3. Hold the extension in the new hand and ease the tiller away, calling "Lee-oh".

4. Put your front foot across the boat and pivot to move into the middle of the boat, <u>facing aft</u>.

5. As the boom passes over your head, turn to sit down on the new side and straighten the tiller as the sail fills.

6. Trim the sails. Tidy up the sheet falls.

WIND

⑤

Duck to avoid swinging boom ④

Helmsman changes hands on main and tiller ③

②

①

The Crew's Role

The crew's job during the tack is to check for obstructions and to move across the boat while setting the jib on the new side.

1. When the helm calls "Ready about", check that the area is clear, uncleat the jib sheet and reply "Ready".

2. Aim to be in the middle of the boat at the same time as the boom. As the boat turns and the jib starts to flap, let go of the old jib sheet and pick up the new one.

3. When the jib has blown across to the new side, pull in the sheet to trim the jib for the new course and balance the boat.

When tacking or gybing a centre-mainsheet boat, <u>face forward</u> and change hands after the tack. In an aft-mainsheet boat, change hands first and <u>face aft</u>.

Tacking a Single-handed Dinghy

Good timing and smooth movements are the keys to tacking a single-handed dinghy. Most have a centre-mainsheet arrangement, so you tack facing forwards. Being small and light, single-handed dinghies turn quickly. At first, aim to tack fairly slowly until you get used to the routine.

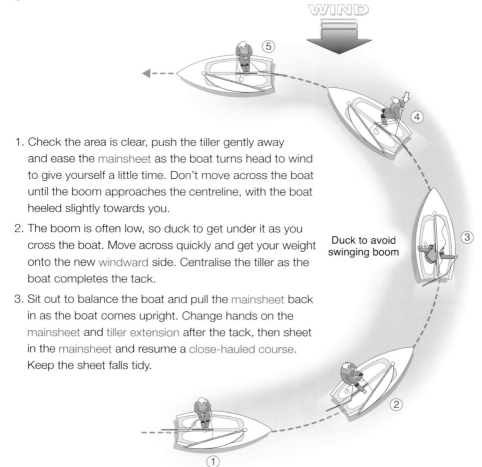

1. Check the area is clear, push the tiller gently away and ease the mainsheet as the boat turns head to wind to give yourself a little time. Don't move across the boat until the boom approaches the centreline, with the boat heeled slightly towards you.

2. The boom is often low, so duck to get under it as you cross the boat. Move across quickly and get your weight onto the new windward side. Centralise the tiller as the boat completes the tack.

Duck to avoid swinging boom

3. Sit out to balance the boat and pull the mainsheet back in as the boat comes upright. Change hands on the mainsheet and tiller extension after the tack, then sheet in the mainsheet and resume a close-hauled course. Keep the sheet falls tidy.

Tacking a Multihull

Tacking a multihull requires a slightly different technique. A multihull's light weight and wide beam causes the boat to stop quickly when it comes head to wind in the middle of the tack. To prevent this, make sure the boat is sailing fast on a close-hauled course before the tack.

The Helm

The checks and communication with the crew are the same as in a dinghy:

1. To start the tack, push the tiller extension to turn the rudders to an angle of about 45°. At the same time, sheet in the mainsail tightly to help the boat turn into the wind.

2. Leading with the front foot, move into the middle and kneel on the trampoline, <u>facing aft</u>. As the mainsheet traveller moves into the centre, rotate the tiller extension aft (behind) the mainsheet. Pass the extension to the other side and change hands on the mainsheet.

3. As soon as the boat passes head to wind, ease the mainsheet a little. Bear away slightly and sheet in until the boat picks up speed, then luff back to close-hauled.

WIND

Duck to avoid sail

④

③

②

①

The Crew

When the boat turns head to wind, allow the jib to back a little (backing the jib – see Backed). This will help the boat turn through the wind without stopping. As the mainsail fills, release the windward sheet and pull in the sail on the leeward side. Move across the boat to the new windward side.

In Irons

When a boat stops head to wind, which can happen during a tack, it is called 'being in irons'. The rudder has no effect because the boat is not moving through the water. To get 'out of irons', push the tiller away from you and push the boom away to back the mainsail. The boat will move backwards and turn away from the wind. Now pull on the tiller and pull on the mainsheet to get the boat sailing again – 'push push, pull pull'.

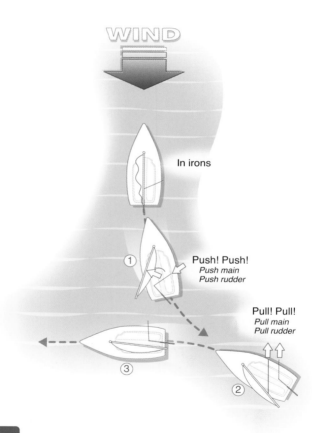

In irons

① Push! Push!
Push main
Push rudder

Pull! Pull!
Pull main
Pull rudder

②

③

TOP TIP

In a boat with a jib, the crew can help recover from in irons by pulling the jib sheet on the side opposite the boom – called backing the jib (see Backed).

8. GYBING

Gybing takes the boat from one tack to the other when sailing downwind by turning the stern through the wind. During a gybe, the sails stay full throughout. Gybing happens more quickly than tacking, and the boom swings across the boat more forcefully, so try and balance the boat throughout the gybe. Raise the centreboard or daggerboard three-quarters up to reduce the heeling effect.

Centre-mainsheet Gybing

Always <u>face forward</u> when gybing a centre-mainsheet boat.

1. Bear away until the jib hangs limply behind the mainsail, then luff up to a training run. This is the best starting point when you are learning to gybe. Check the area is clear and pull the boom off the leeward shroud. Check the centreboard is one-third up. Call "Stand by to gybe". Rotate the tiller extension to the leeward side. Place your back foot across the boat, moving to the middle.

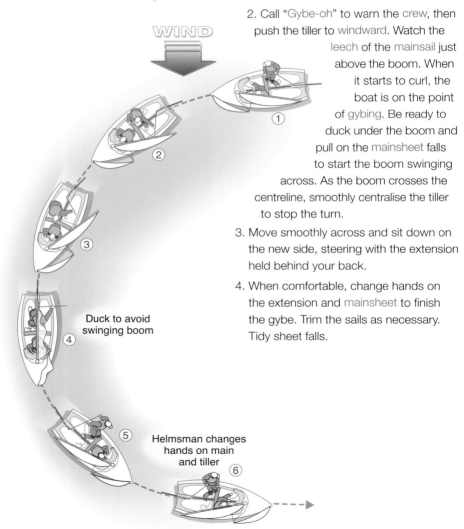

WIND

Duck to avoid
swinging boom

Helmsman changes
hands on main
and tiller

2. Call "Gybe-oh" to warn the crew, then push the tiller to windward. Watch the leech of the mainsail just above the boom. When it starts to curl, the boat is on the point of gybing. Be ready to duck under the boom and pull on the mainsheet falls to start the boom swinging across. As the boom crosses the centreline, smoothly centralise the tiller to stop the turn.

3. Move smoothly across and sit down on the new side, steering with the extension held behind your back.

4. When comfortable, change hands on the extension and mainsheet to finish the gybe. Trim the sails as necessary. Tidy sheet falls.

Aft-mainsheet Gybing

Gybing with an aft mainsheet is slightly different. As with tacking, you change hands on the mainsheet and tiller extension before the gybe and cross the boat facing aft.

1. Do the pre-gybe checks, including checking the area is clear, and warn the crew you are about to gybe by calling "Stand by to gybe". Change hands on the mainsheet and extension. Call "Gybe-oh" and push the tiller to windward to start the turn.

2. Leading with the front foot, move to the middle of the boat, facing aft. Be ready to duck to avoid the boom. Watch the leech of the mainsail just above the boom. When it starts to curl, the boat is on the point of gybing. Give a tug on the mainsheet to start the boom moving.

3. Centralise the tiller to stop the boat turning as the boom crosses the centreline.

4. Sit down on the new side and trim the sails. Tidy sheet falls.

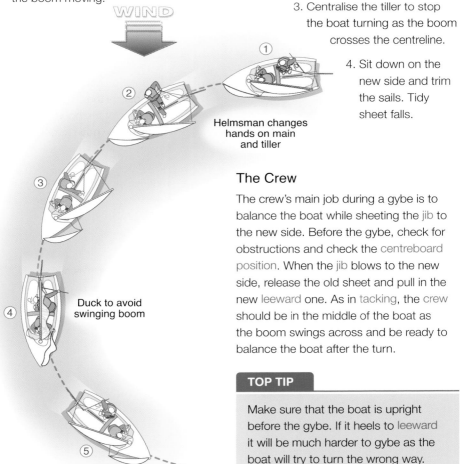

Helmsman changes hands on main and tiller

Duck to avoid swinging boom

The Crew

The crew's main job during a gybe is to balance the boat while sheeting the jib to the new side. Before the gybe, check for obstructions and check the centreboard position. When the jib blows to the new side, release the old sheet and pull in the new leeward one. As in tacking, the crew should be in the middle of the boat as the boom swings across and be ready to balance the boat after the turn.

> **TOP TIP**
>
> Make sure that the boat is upright before the gybe. If it heels to leeward it will be much harder to gybe as the boat will try to turn the wrong way.

Gybing a Single-handed Dinghy

In a single-handed dinghy you have sole responsibility for balancing the boat, so plan your gybe in advance. Ease the kicking strap a little before the gybe, thus lifting the boom. This will reduce the risk of the end of the boom hitting the water when it comes across.

Pull the daggerboard nearly all the way up, but not so far that the top could be snagged by the kicking strap during the gybe. The faster you go the easier it is to gybe, so wait until the boat is moving well. Most single-handed dinghies have a centre mainsheet, so gybe facing forward.

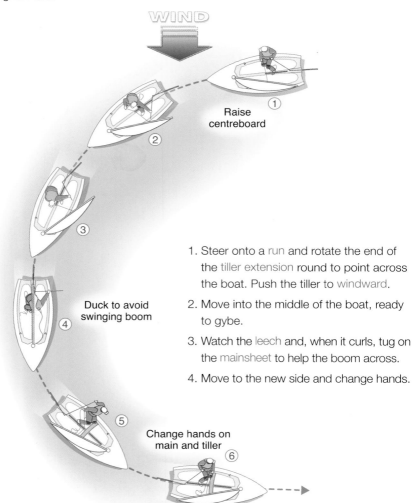

Raise centreboard

Duck to avoid swinging boom

Change hands on main and tiller

1. Steer onto a run and rotate the end of the tiller extension round to point across the boat. Push the tiller to windward.

2. Move into the middle of the boat, ready to gybe.

3. Watch the leech and, when it curls, tug on the mainsheet to help the boom across.

4. Move to the new side and change hands.

Gybing a Multihull

Multihulls are usually easier to gybe due to their stability; however, its extra speed means that you need plenty of clear sailing area. To manoeuvre, the boat should be under full control before you start the gybe.

The Helm

The checks and communication with the crew are the same as in a two-man dinghy. If your multihull has centreboards or daggerboards they should be fully raised.

1. Start the gybe by pulling the tiller extension to turn the rudders.

2. Move to the middle of the boat as it turns onto a run and kneel, facing aft. Keep the rudders over to continue the turn and rotate the tiller extension aft. Swing the tiller extension behind the mainsheet to the other side and change hands on the mainsheet and extension.

3. With your new mainsheet hand, grasp the mainsheet falls. As the sail swings across, briefly check the mainsheet's movement to leeward. This will cause the sail's full-length battens to 'pop' across on the new tack. Straighten the rudders.

4. Sit down on the windward hull and steer onto your new course.

The Crew

A multihull's stability makes it easy for the crew to balance the boat. Before the gybe, check that the route is clear. If your boat has centreboards or daggerboards, make sure that they are raised. Respond with "Ready". Uncleat the old jib sheet and pick up the new one. When the jib crosses to the new side, release the jib sheet, pull in the other one, and move to the new windward side.

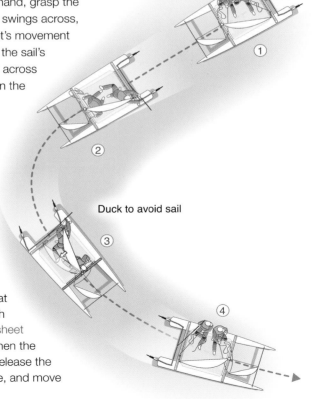

Duck to avoid sail

The Five Essentials

There are five essential factors to sailing a boat efficiently. Whenever one factor changes, check the other four to make sure they are still correct.

- Sail trim – Constantly check that the sails are set properly by either using the tell-tales or slowly letting out the sails until they start to flap along the luff, then pulling them in again until the flapping just stops.
- Centreboard position – The daggerboard or centreboard position needs to be adjusted according to the side force. The amount of side force and centreboard required varies according to the point of sailing we are on. On a keelboat you cannot adjust the area.
- Boat balance – Most boats sail fastest when upright. This is achieved by the crew moving their weight to balance the boat. When sailing close-hauled the board will heel, so the helm and crew need to sit out to keep the boat upright. As we bear away the heeling reduces, so the crew moves to the opposite side of the boat to balance the helmsman's weight.
- Boat trim – Generally, the boat should be level fore and aft. Depending on the conditions, the helmsman and crew sit close together and avoid depressing the bow or stern excessively.
- Course – Keep checking your course and the best route to your destination. If your target is to windward anywhere in the no-go zone, you will have to zig-zag upwind to get there.

TOP TIP

The sails have a big turning effect, so when you want to bear away let out the mainsail first. To luff up, pull the mainsail in as you turn.

9. KNOTS & ROPEWORK

Ropes are an essential part of a sailing boat and, while many racing boats have quite complex control systems, you only need to know a few knots to cope with most needs. Modern ropes are incredibly strong and light, and come in a wide range of sizes. Use low-stretch rope for sheets, halyards and control lines with the length just long enough for the job so the rope doesn't tangle.

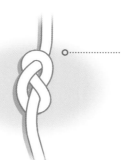

Figure-of-eight

The figure-of-eight is used to put a stopper knot in the end of rope to stop it running out through a fairlead or turning block.

Round Turn & Two Half-hitches

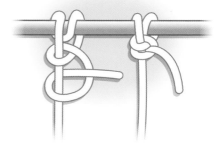

The round turn and two half-hitches is a secure knot that is used to tie to a post or ring.

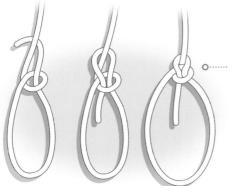

Bowline

The bowline is used to make a loop in a rope or to tie to a ring or post. It is a secure knot but cannot be untied when under load.

Clove Hitch ·····································o

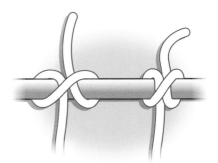

A clove hitch can be used to tie a rope to a
post or ring. It is quick to tie but a snatching
load can undo it, so leave a long working end.

Rolling Hitch

The rolling hitch is more secure than the clove hitch and will not slide along another rope
or a spar. It is useful when you need to take the load off another rope.

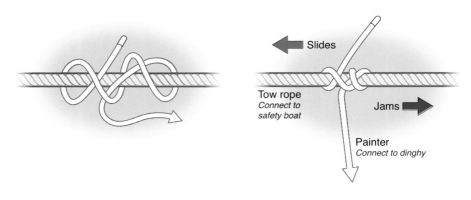

Slides

Tow rope
*Connect to
safety boat*

Jams

Painter
Connect to dinghy

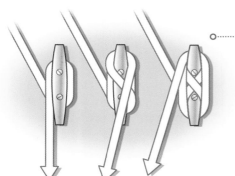

o······· # Using a Cleat

Take the rope to the back of the cleat and
make a full turn around it. Then make two
or three full figure-of eight turns around the
cleat before taking another full turn around it.

Using Winches

Keelboats tend to use winches to help with the heavy loads on sheets and halyards.

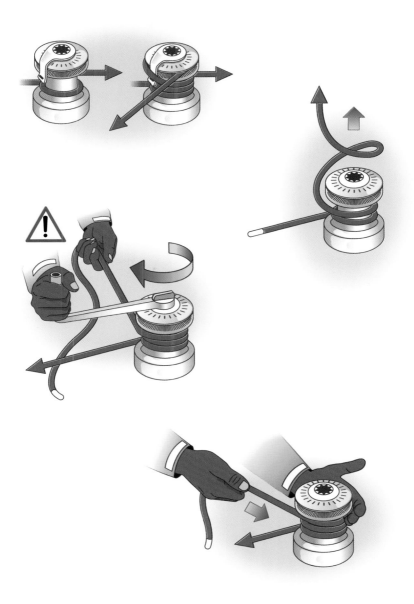

10. LEAVING & RETURNING TO SHORE

Wind Awareness

It is much easier to learn key manoeuvres once you have developed good awareness of wind direction. The wind is constantly changing, so check its direction regularly. Flags ashore at the centre or club will give a general idea of wind direction before getting afloat, but the best indicator is the feel of wind on your face and neck and the set of the sails. With a little practice, you will soon develop an automatic awareness of wind direction.

Wind Direction

There are two main ways of referring to wind direction:

1. Using the points of the compass – the wind direction describes where the wind is coming from. For example, a southerly wind is when the wind is blowing from the south.

2. Relative to the shoreline – wind direction can be described as onshore, cross-shore or offshore. Combinations of these terms are also used, e.g.: cross-onshore.

Make sure that you take transits and look for a landing point directly downwind of where you are sailing in case you are unable to stay upwind!

The one wind direction to avoid is offshore. It can be dangerous unless properly supervised at an RYA Recognised Training Centre, as you may even get blown right out to sea.

The wind strength may seem light and the water may look calm next to the shore, but further out the wind will almost certainly be a lot stronger and the water will get progressively rougher – not good conditions for you to improve your skills!

DOWNWIND

WIND

Offshore Wind
(weather shore)

Cross-shore Wind

Onshore Wind
(lee shore)

UPWIND

Sailing to and from the shore is straightforward if you understand the importance of wind direction. When the wind is blowing along the shore (cross-shore) you can easily sail away and return on a beam reach. More often the wind blows off the shore (windward shore) or onto the shore (lee shore).

Onshore Winds (Lee Shore)

Before launching, turn the boat head to wind and hoist the jib, hoisting the mainsail once afloat. In a single-handed dinghy, rig ashore and get a friend to help you launch.

To leave a lee shore push off, climb aboard and steer onto a close reach until you reach water deep enough to lower the centreboard and rudder fully, sailing close-hauled to get away from the shore.

WIND

③ Close reach

Lower centreboard and rudder.
Set sails

②

Hold boat head to wind

①

Helm climbs aboard

To return to a lee shore turn head to wind just offshore, lower the mainsail and sail in using the jib alone. In a single-handed dinghy, sail in and, if the bottom is gently shelving, turn head to wind near the shore and step out.

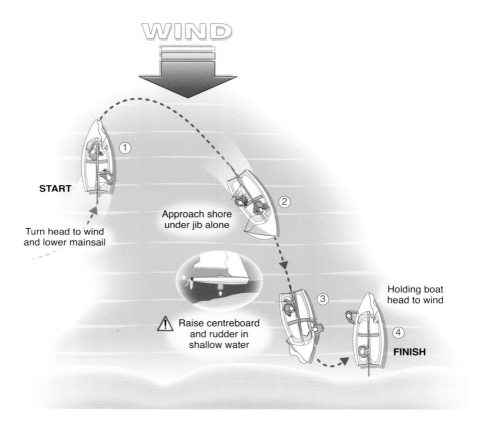

WIND

(1)

START

Turn head to wind
and lower mainsail

Approach shore
under jib alone

(2)

⚠ Raise centreboard
and rudder in
shallow water

(3)

Holding boat
head to wind

(4)

FINISH

On a steeply shelving shore sail straight in but turn the boat into the wind (luff) to depower the sail and jump out on the windward side when the water is shallow enough.

Waves break on a lee shore in moderate or strong winds and make launching harder and recovery more difficult. If the shoreline shelves steeply it may be unsafe to launch, so find a better launching site.

Offshore Winds (Windward)

It is often deceptively calm on a windward shore but there may be stronger winds offshore. Be cautious in case you start with too much sail. Launch the boat with the sails hoisted before sailing away on a broad reach or run.

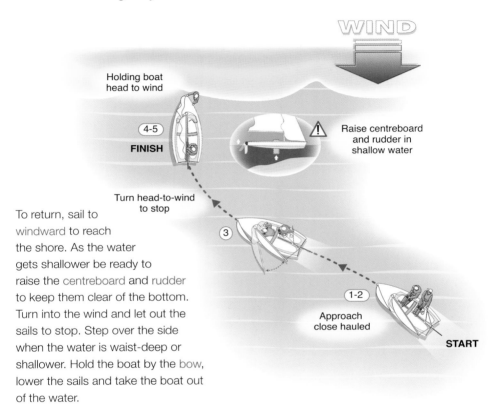

Holding boat head to wind

4-5

FINISH

Raise centreboard and rudder in shallow water

Turn head-to-wind to stop

To return, sail to windward to reach the shore. As the water gets shallower be ready to raise the centreboard and rudder to keep them clear of the bottom. Turn into the wind and let out the sails to stop. Step over the side when the water is waist-deep or shallower. Hold the boat by the bow, lower the sails and take the boat out of the water.

3

Approach close hauled

1-2

START

Towing

To get to and from the sailing area boats can be towed one behind the other. Lower the sails, pull the centreboard right up and remove the rudder, sitting near the stern to lift the bow.

The last boat in the tow keeps its rudder fitted and steers to follow the boat directly ahead. In a single-handed dinghy remove the boom, allowing the mainsail to flap freely, or roll the sail up.

11. CAPSIZING

Knowing how to deal with a capsize is an important part of learning to sail small boats. At an RYA Recognised Training Centre you will be taught how to handle a capsize, learning the simple techniques for righting the boat and gaining confidence for dealing with the real situation. Once you have mastered a recovery technique that works well for your type of boat, a capsize will usually be little more than an inconvenience from which you can quickly recover.

TOP TIP

If you find yourself in the water under a sail, just put your hand above your head to create an airspace and swim to the sail's edge.

Righting a Two-person Boat

The most common type of capsize occurs when the boat heels too much and capsizes to leeward. This type of capsize is relatively slow and gentle. Remember, your buoyancy aid will keep you afloat so just relax and communicate with your helm/crew.

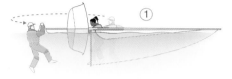

1. As the boat falls onto its side, helm and crew lower themselves into the water between the hull and the sail. Both helm and crew work their way to the stern and check that the rudder is secure and has not floated off.

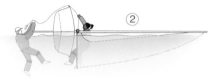

2. The helmsman takes the end of the mainsheet as a safety line and swims round the hull to the centreboard, checking it is fully down. If not, the crew can push it down. If the helmsman is very light the crew may go to the centreboard.

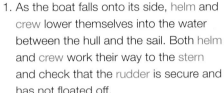

3. The crew now moves back into the boat and finds the end of the upper jib sheet, throwing it over the hull to the helmsman.

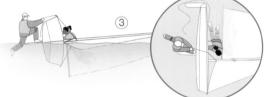

4. Once he or she has the jib sheet, the helmsman lets go of the mainsheet and climbs onto the centreboard. The crew floats inside the boat, holding on to a toestrap and checking the mainsheet is free. The helmsman now stands with his or her feet near the hull and leans back on the jib sheet.

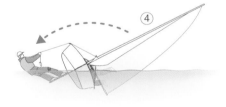

5. The mast and sails will slowly start to lift from the water as the boat comes upright. The crew will be scooped aboard and can help the helmsman into the boat over the side or stern.

Righting from an Inversion

Any boat will turn completely upside down if left on its side for long. This is known as inversion. Some boats are more prone to this than others.

1. The first step in recovering is to bring the boat back onto its side. Pull yourself onto the upturned hull and stand on the edge while leaning back against the centreboard. If the centreboard has retracted into its case, use a sheet from the other side of the boat to pull against.

2. Now use the standard righting method. If you have to right an inverted multihull, sit on the stern of the leeward hull until the opposite bow lifts and the mast starts to come to the surface. As it does so, move to the middle of the lower hull and continue the normal righting process.

3. Masthead flotation is used on most two-person training dinghies to stop boats from inverting.

Righting a Single-hander

Righting a single-hander is easy if you can climb over the high side and onto the centreboard as the boat goes over. From here you can quickly pull the boat upright and climb aboard, staying dry throughout the process!

If the boat capsizes quickly and you can't climb over the high side, or if the boat capsizes to windward, lower yourself gently into the water. Use the mainsheet as a safety line and swim round the hull to the centreboard. To right the boat, pull on the centreboard, or climb onto it. As you pull on the side of the hull the boat will right itself and you can climb aboard.

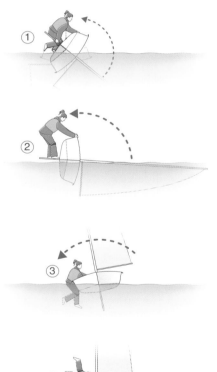

Righting a Multihull

As the multihull capsizes, slide into the water between the trampoline and the sail. Keep hold of something – the boat may drift quite fast. Once capsized, a multihull can be harder to right than a dinghy, especially if it turns upside down.

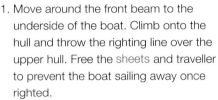

1. Move around the front beam to the underside of the boat. Climb onto the hull and throw the righting line over the upper hull. Free the sheets and traveller to prevent the boat sailing away once righted.

2. Turn the boat so that the mast points into wind (the opposite to a dinghy) – the windage of the trampoline and rig will help you right the boat. If necessary, gently depress the bow to swing the hulls around in the breeze. Lean back on the righting line (or sheet) to lift the mast tip clear of the water. When the mast lifts clear, the wind will get under the sail, lifting it. The boat will start to right more quickly.

3. Stay under the boat by the front beam as the top hull drops back into the water. Be careful it does not hit you. Grab the front beam as it comes down. This will prevent the boat sailing off or capsizing again.

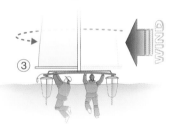

4. Climb aboard over either beam, check the rudder and sheets and stow any loose lines. Climbing over the lower rear beam is easier if you are tired.

TOP TIP

Many boats will drift faster than you can swim when on their side, so always keep hold of the boat when you are in the water.

12. MAN OVERBOARD RECOVERY

Man overboard does not happen very often but, if it does, these simple steps will help. If you are sailing a two-person dinghy or multihull when the other person falls overboard, your first priority is to get the boat under control and to avoid a capsize.

If you are helming and your crew falls overboard, <u>let go of the jib sheet immediately</u>. If you are crew and the helmsman falls out of the boat, <u>release the jib sheet and grab the tiller to gain control</u>.

If the boat capsizes, you may be close enough for the person in the water to swim to the boat. If not, you must try and right the boat while keeping the person in the water in sight. **Never leave the boat to try and reach them.**

Once you have the boat under control:

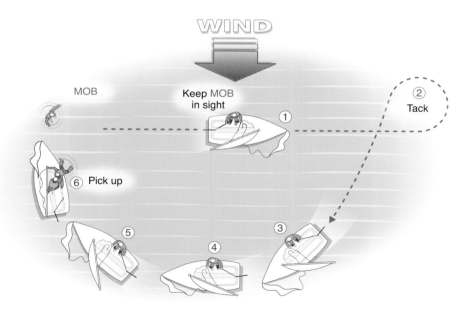

1. Steer onto a beam reach and check the position of the person in the water.
2. Let the jib sheet go and ease the mainsail sufficiently to keep the boat upright while retaining enough speed to manoeuvre.

3. Sail away from the person in the water until you have enough room to get downwind of them. Ten boat lengths is typical.

4. Check that both jib sheets are loose and tack round to the opposite beam reach. Check that you have the person in sight and bear away to a broad reach to get to leeward of them.

5. Make your final approach on a close reach so you can slow down by letting out the mainsheet without the boom hitting the shroud. The flapping jib is a useful indicator of wind direction.

6. Aim to stop with the person alongside the windward shroud.

In a multihull you can gybe round to avoid getting stuck in irons trying to tack. In strong winds, aim to stop the boat with the person between the bows. This prevents the boat blowing away from the person in the water as the boat slows down.

Getting the Person Aboard

As the boat stops alongside the person in the water, let the mainsheet run out fully and move forward to grab hold of them. If the boat is still moving it may try to tack around the person in the water, so give the tiller extension a tug to windward as you leave it. To get the person out of the water:

1. Kneel at the side of the boat and hold the person by their buoyancy aid or under their armpits.

2. Lean towards them to depress the side of the boat. Then lean backwards and pull their torso over the side.

3. From here, most people can help themselves aboard. If not, have them float alongside the boat, get one of their feet into the boat, then roll their torso aboard horizontally.

4. In a multihull, bring the person aboard over the forward beam or, if too difficult, over the aft beam where the freeboard is less.

TOP TIP

When making the final approach, sail slowly and allow the jib to flap. Luff onto a close reach well before the line of the jib points at the person in the water.

13. MOORINGS & PONTOONS

Picking up a Mooring

In many locations moorings are used to provide temporary or permanent berths for keelboats and larger dinghies. A mooring is normally a floating buoy tethered fast to the bottom. Head for a mooring on a close reach, letting out the sails to slow the boat down as you approach. Turn almost head to wind, stopping alongside the buoy, and secure the boat to the buoy. Raise the centreboard, lower the sails and remove the rudder (see diagram A).

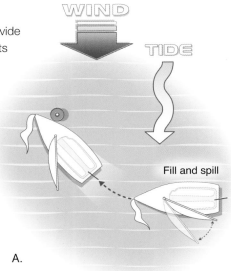

Fill and spill

A.

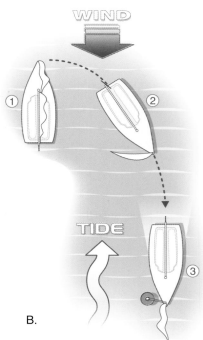

B.

In tidal waters, take account of the direction of the current. If wind and tide are in the same direction, follow diagram A. If wind and tide are opposed, follow diagram B – drop the mainsail and approach under jib alone. Note that you must have enough speed under jib to get over the tide.

Using an Engine

Some dinghies and small keelboats may have the facility to use an engine. This is usually a small outboard that clamps onto the transom. Ensure that it is clamped tightly to its bracket and check that it is not in gear before you start it. Do not use an engine near swimmers or people stood in shallow water. Remember to lower the sails when under power and pull up the centreboard.

Tying up to a Pontoon

A floating pontoon can be convenient as a temporary stop or a permanent home for a dinghy or keelboat. When approaching a pontoon under sail, come in on a close reach, letting the sails out to slow down the final approach. There are two golden rules when approaching a pontoon:

1. Always moderate your speed to reduce the risk of collision and increase control.

2. Always plan an escape route so that if you find yourself sailing too fast in the final stages you can sail out and try again.

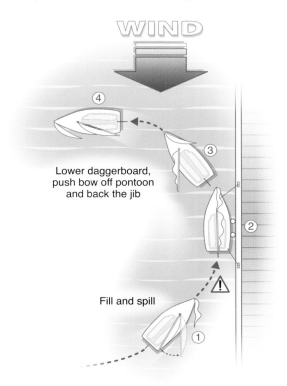

Lower daggerboard, push bow off pontoon and back the jib

Fill and spill

As you reach the pontoon, turn head to wind to stop. If this is not possible, approach under jib alone. Secure the boat and lower the sails. Tie the bow and stern to the pontoon.

To leave the pontoon, hoist the sails, untie the boat, push the bow off and sail away.

If you sail a keelboat, secure the boat alongside the pontoon using two sets of ropes. The ropes from the bow and stern will hold the boat close to the pontoon and are called breast ropes. The others are called springs and they stop the boat moving fore and aft. Tie some fenders at the widest part of the boat to stop it rubbing against the pontoon.

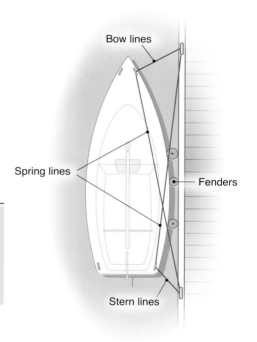

Bow lines

Spring lines

Fenders

Stern lines

TOP TIP

Don't leave your dinghy tied to a pontoon for long, as the action of the waves can cause damage to the hull by banging it against the pontoon. Always use a fender.

14. BASIC THEORY

Understanding how a Boat Works

How Sails Work

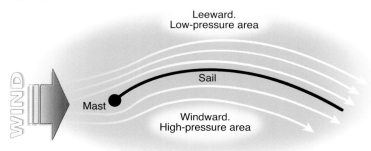

Leeward.
Low-pressure area

Sail

Mast

Windward.
High-pressure area

WIND

To understand how a sail works, try a simple experiment with a spoon under a running tap.

Hold the spoon lightly by the handle and move the back of the spoon slowly towards the stream of water. You would expect it to be pushed away by the water but actually the spoon is sucked into the flow. The same thing happens when air flows around a sail. The air travelling around the outside (leeward side) of the sail moves faster round the sail than the air on the windward side. This causes a difference in pressure on the two sides of the sail which pulls it to leeward. The force created by the sail acts roughly at right angles to the boom but only part of it drives the boat forward – the rest tries to push it sideways.

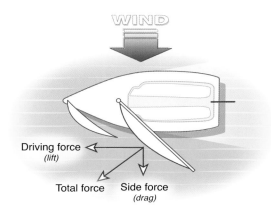

WIND

Driving force
(lift)

Total force   Side force
(drag)

Trimming Sails

A sail works best when its leading edge (the luff) is held at a small angle to the wind. The angle is critical but there is a simple way to find it. Watch the luff of the sail as you pull in the sheet.

Windward tell-tale higher

(Sheet in)

Stop pulling when the luff stops flapping. To check that the sail is properly trimmed, slowly let out the sheet until the luff starts to flap, then pull it in again until the flapping stops. Most jibs and some mainsails have tell-tales. These are fitted near the luff, on each side of the sail, and help to trim the sail accurately.

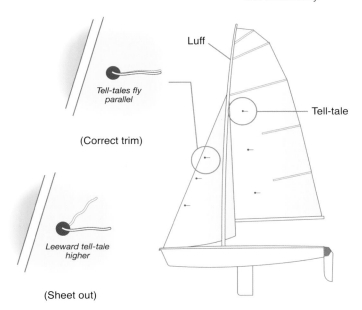

Tell-tales fly parallel

(Correct trim)

Luff

Tell-tale

Leeward tell-tale higher

(Sheet out)

How Keels, Centreboards and Daggerboards Work

A boat's keel, centreboard, or daggerboard is designed to resist the sideways force created by the sails. The rudder also plays a part. When the boat starts to move, water flows across the centreboard in much the same way as air flows across the sail. It creates a sideways force to windward that resists the opposite force on the sail. The two sideways forces cancel each other out, leaving a forward force which drives the boat. The force on the sails acts roughly at right angles to the boom. With sails in tight (when sailing close to the wind) the force acts mainly in a sideways direction. More sideways resistance is therefore required from the daggerboard. This is why most dinghies and some multihulls have a lifting centreboard or daggerboard, so that the area under the boat can be adjusted to suit the point of sailing.

WIND

Centreboard
(down)

Track

Boat slips
to leeward

Centreboard
(raised)

Staying Upright

The wind in the sail and the force created by the daggerboard acts under the boat, creating a heeling force. If this force is too great, the boat may capsize. Keelboats use the weight of a fixed keel to keep them upright, while dinghies and multihulls rely on the weight and position of the crew.

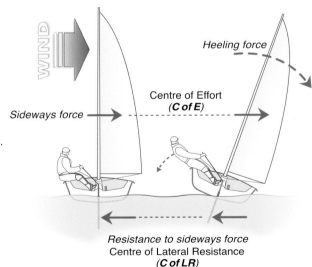

WIND

Heeling force

Sideways force

Centre of Effort
(C of E)

Resistance to sideways force
Centre of Lateral Resistance
(C of LR)

TOP TIP

All sails work best when they are pulled in just enough to stop the flapping at the luff – any more will slow the boat down.

15. AVOIDING OTHER BOATS

Popular sailing areas can get very busy so it is important to understand the rules for avoiding collisions. These rules are called the International Regulations for Preventing Collisions at Sea.

Your principal duty is to avoid hitting anything, so keep a good look out at all times. As a beginner it is always better to slow or stop the boat by letting the sheets go and turning into the wind, rather than increasing momentum by turning away from the wind.

Under Sail

'STARBOARD TACK IS THE STAND-ON VESSEL': A sailing boat on port tack must keep clear of a boat on starboard tack. If you are on starboard tack, hold your course but be watchful in case the 'port boat' has not seen you. Remember, starboard tack is the wind coming from the right-hand side of the boat.

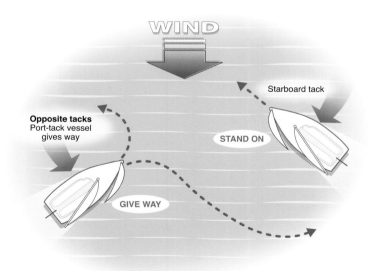

'WINDWARD BOAT KEEPS CLEAR':
When boats are on the same
tack, the boat to windward
keeps clear.

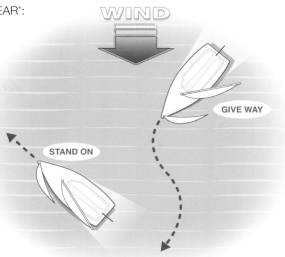

GIVE WAY

STAND ON

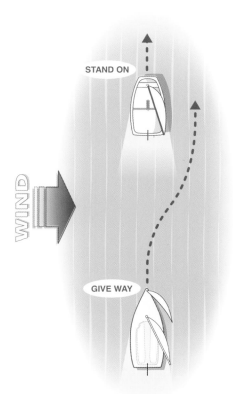

STAND ON

WIND

GIVE WAY

'OVERTAKING BOAT KEEPS CLEAR':
If you are overtaking another boat you
must keep clear, even if you are sailing
past a power vessel.

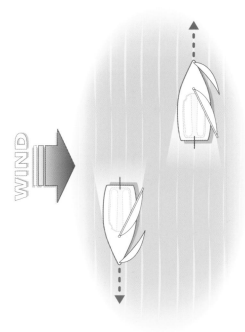

'DRIVE ON THE RIGHT': When sailing up or down a narrow channel, always 'drive on the right' – whether under power or sail – and stay on the right-hand side of the channel. If you cross the channel, do so at right angles and give way to all boats following the channel.

'POWER GIVES WAY TO SAIL': Beware! It is unrealistic to expect large powered vessels to give way to a small sailing boat and in many cases it is your duty to give way. Use your common sense and take early and clear avoiding action.

Under Power

Whether rowing, paddling or using the engine you are considered to be under power, so be aware of your responsibilities. This applies even if the sails are hoisted.

'BOATS UNDER POWER': When two boats under power meet head on they must both turn to starboard, so they pass port side to port side.

TOP TIP

To help you remember which tack you are on, write 'port' and 'starboard' on your boom!

16. BASIC WEATHER

The Causes of Weather

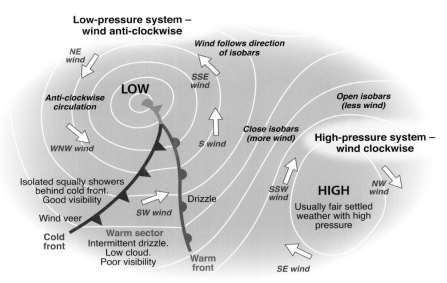

Northern Hemisphere

Low-pressure system – wind anti-clockwise

Wind follows direction of isobars

NE wind

SSE wind

LOW

Anti-clockwise circulation

Open isobars (less wind)

WNW wind

Close isobars (more wind)

S wind

High-pressure system – wind clockwise

Isolated squally showers behind cold front. Good visibility

SSW wind

HIGH

NW wind

Wind veer

SW wind

Drizzle

Usually fair settled weather with high pressure

Cold front

Warm sector
Intermittent drizzle.
Low cloud.
Poor visibility

Warm front

SE wind

Weather is a key consideration when you go sailing. Before you go afloat you should know the predicted wind strength and direction, and understand how any local effects may alter the forecast. The weather we experience in the UK is largely determined by Atlantic depressions and is caused by two types of weather systems: low-pressure systems (called depressions or lows) and high-pressure systems (highs or anticyclones).

Low-pressure systems travel across the Atlantic and are associated with strong winds, rain and shifting wind direction. They also feature warm and cold fronts, the dividing lines between warm and cold air. Fronts are associated with changes in wind direction and often gusty conditions.

High-pressure systems are born over land or sea and move more slowly, generally being associated with good weather and light winds.

Local Effects

Wind often differs from what has been forecast, which can be very frustrating. Two sailors discussing their day on the water may find that they have had very different experiences even though they were sailing only a few miles away from each other.

Such differences can be due to the geography of the land, especially on large waters surrounded by hills producing their own localised climatic effects. In some wind directions this can produce funnelling (venturi effects). For example, a prevailing Force 2 wind squeezed between two hills can exit the end of the valley at twice the strength. This kind of knowledge can usually only be gained from local sailors. As you start to sail regularly at alternative locations, in different conditions, you will soon pick up on the local knowledge and become a better informed and competent sailor.

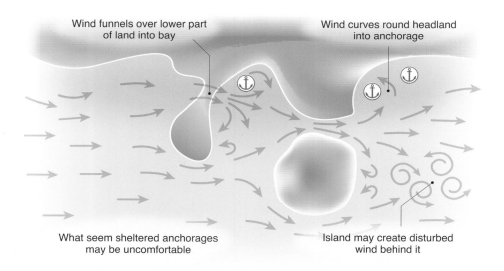

Wind funnels over lower part of land into bay

Wind curves round headland into anchorage

What seem sheltered anchorages may be uncomfortable

Island may create disturbed wind behind it

Sea Breeze

There are other local effects that can cause the weather to vary from the forecast. For example, on bright summer days when the wind is light in the morning, there's a good chance of a sea breeze later on in the day. A sea breeze is a thermal wind generated by the temperature difference between the land and the sea. As the land warms up throughout the day, warm air rises up from the land. This air is replaced by cooler air drawn off the sea which may generate a brisk onshore wind, either in the same or a different direction to that forecast. This effect tends to peak by mid-afternoon and can reach a good Force 4.

The presence of strong sunshine is not a guarantee of a sea breeze, as even a light local wind can sometimes destroy this effect. A tell-tale sign that a sea breeze is on its way is the formation of light, fluffy clouds over the coast. This means that hot air is rising and condensing.

For more in-depth knowledge on weather patterns, check out the RYA Weather Handbook.

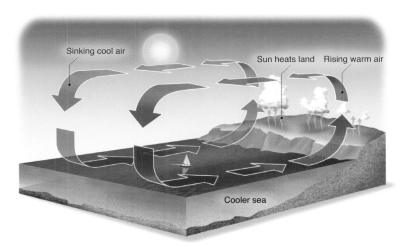

Sinking cool air

Sun heats land   Rising warm air

Cooler sea

Getting a Forecast

You do not need detailed knowledge of weather to go sailing but it is important to get a forecast. Check the forecast for wind strength and direction as well as poor visibility or fog. Good sources of information include various websites, radio, television, and phone.

TOP TIP

Check out the local weather forecast before you go sailing and ask advice from experienced locals if you are not sure about the conditions.

Wind Strength and the Beaufort Scale

Wind strength is described in the Beaufort Scale below. Learn to recognise the strength of the wind by what you see ashore and afloat.

Force	Wind Speed	Description	Signs on Land	Effects on Sea
0	Less than 1 knot	Calm	Flags hang limply, leaves do not move on trees, smoke rises vertically.	Glassy sea, boats drift with limp sails. Heel the boat to leeward a little to help the sails hold their shape. Move gently and slowly in the boat.
1	1–3 knots	Light Air	Light flags start to stir and smoke drifts away from vertical.	Small catspaws and ripples on surface, and sails fill. Sit forward in the boat and allow it to heel slightly to keep sails full. Move gently in the boat.
2	4–6 knots	Light Breeze	Flags start to indicate wind direction and leaves rustle on trees.	Steady light wind for sailing. Boats are still underpowered but can be sailed upright. Use smooth movements during manoeuvres to maintain speed.
3	7–10 knots	Gentle Breeze	Flags extend outwards but remain below horizontal from the flagstaff.	Ideal conditions for learning to sail. Small waves form and most small boats sail efficiently with full power available from the sails.
4	11–16 knots	Moderate Breeze	Small branches move on trees, flags are fully extended horizontally. Small pieces of paper blow along the ground.	Waves have foaming tops. Crews have to work hard to balance dinghies and multihulls. Beginners should reef or head for shore.
5	17–21 knots	Fresh Breeze	The tops of large trees move and small trees sway. Flags are extended slightly above horizontal.	Good conditions for experienced crews but capsizes are common. Inexperienced sailors should stay ashore.
6	22–27 knots	Strong Breeze	Wind whistles through telephone lines and large trees sway. Flags blow above horizontal.	Experienced crews may sail but only if good safety cover is available.

17. COASTAL SAILING

Safety Matters – The Seven Common Senses

Before you go out and during your on-water session you should:

• Check the conditions   • Check your equipment   • Check yourself

1. Is all your equipment seaworthy and suitable?

Clothing: Make sure you are wearing suitable clothing to keep you warm and comfortable during your sailing session.

The most common cause of need for rescue is component failure.

Boat and rigging: Check the integrity of the boat's hull and rig, ensuring all ropes are secure and in good condition.

Essential Spares: You should carry with you spare rigging/tow line and a means of attracting attention, such as a whistle.

2. Tell someone where you are going and when you will be back.

It is recommended that you always sail at a venue that has safety provision and, as an extra safety precaution, always ensure that a responsible person knows that you have gone on the water and that you have returned.

3. Obtain a forecast for the local sailing area.

To avoid being caught out by changing conditions, get a forecast. If you are sailing at a new location it is advisable to seek advice from experienced local sailors.

4. Are you capable of handling prevailing conditions?

Ensure you are adequately experienced to handle the conditions you are going out in. Developing your skills in more challenging conditions should be done at a safe location which ideally has safety provision. If in doubt, don't go out.

5. Sail with others.

It's more fun to sail with others. Not only do you learn from a sailing buddy but there will always be someone close by should you need a hand.

6. Avoid strong tides, offshore winds and poor visibility.

Offshore winds and strong tidal streams can sweep you away from the safety of your chosen sailing area. It is essential that you understand the conditions you are sailing in and what consequences could occur.

Poor visibility is best avoided as it prevents you from seeing dangers and others from seeing you should you get into difficulty.

(continued)

7. Consider other water users.

Many sailing locations are busy with other water users. You should respect others on the water by giving them space and taking all necessary action to avoid collision.

Safety Equipment

Sailing is generally a very safe sport but, if you decide to sail in a location that is not an RYA Recognised Training Centre with designated safety cover, it is important to carry the appropriate safety equipment and know how to summon assistance if necessary.

The type and amount of gear you need will depend on the boat you sail and where you go afloat. A paddle to get you home if the wind drops may suffice if you sail on inland waters. If you sail on coastal waters, carry an anchor with sufficient line in case of a breakdown or lack of wind. Folding anchors are the easiest to stow on a small boat.

If your boat is fitted with an engine or gas-fuelled cooking equipment you should have a fire extinguisher on board. A small first-aid kit stowed in a waterproof container is useful in case an injury needs treatment before you can get ashore. Whatever equipment you carry, keep it in good condition and make sure that you know how to use it.

How to Summon Help

If a situation develops beyond the point where you can deal with it, seek outside assistance. If you sail on inland waters you may be able to attract attention by shouting. If you sail on coastal waters carry flares and keep them dry. Read the instructions and explain to your crew how to use the flares before the need arises.

Sailing in Coastal Waters

Coastal waters provide some wonderful sailing venues with the opportunity for good racing or day sailing. Care should always be taken as waves can develop quickly on the sea when the wind reaches Force 3 or more, especially in open waters.

Before you go afloat in coastal waters, check the weather forecast for several hours ahead and ensure that the conditions will be within your capabilities. Additionally, check the time of high and low water, and find out the direction of the tidal stream during the time you plan to be sailing.

You can find the times of high and low water in a local tide table, and the direction of the tidal stream from a pilot guide, tidal atlas or chart of the area. It is best to sail from an RYA Recognised Training Centre but, if you do go out, if you are in any doubt, ask an experienced local sailor for advice. Tell a reliable person of your plans and the time you expect to be back so they can notify the rescue services if you do not return on time.

Tides

Whatever your level, as soon as you go sailing in the sea you need knowledge of both general tidal effects and local tidal characteristics. An understanding of tides plays an essential role in making sailing safe and enjoyable.

Tidal Movement

The two elements to tides affect sailors – vertical and horizontal movements.

Vertical Movement

The movement of water up and down a beach or sea wall is known as tidal range. Vertical movement varies daily and from area to area. When the water is rising, the tide is coming in or flooding. When the water is falling, the tide is going out or ebbing.

The difference between high and low water is approximately six hours. The rate of flow between high and low water can be generalised by the 'Rule of Twelfths'. The diagram below illustrates how much water flows during a given hour.

The greatest movement of water is during the middle two hours and the least either side of low and high water.

If we take the two middle hours – the third and fourth hours – we can see that 6/12ths or half of the water will flow during this time. This shows that during this time frame we experience the fastest tidal flow.

You will notice that, during hours one and six, only 1/12th of the water will flow during each of these times. Therefore, this is the slowest tidal movement during the six-hour period.

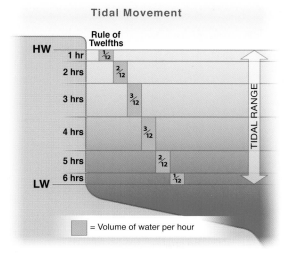

Tidal Movement

= Volume of water per hour

You can find out what the vertical tides are doing and how they will affect your local coastal venue by using tide timetables (tide tables), available via the internet, almanacs, and harbour offices.

In some extreme locations a strongly ebbing tide could pull a sailor out to sea, but at most coastal locations such tidal movements simply mean that the sea level rises and falls. When it does fall there may not be enough water left for you to continue sailing!

Horizontal Movement

This effect of the tide flooding or ebbing is a parallel movement along the coastline, usually called tidal stream. As we have seen through the Rule of Twelfths, the rate of water flow varies throughout the time period between high and low water. More specific information about tidal streams is found in a tidal stream atlas.

When choosing a new sailing location on coastal waters, knowledge of the rate and direction of the tidal stream is important as this can affect your position on the water. When out on the water, transits can be taken which help you to check your position visually. The taking of transits can also help you to understand the strength of the tidal stream.

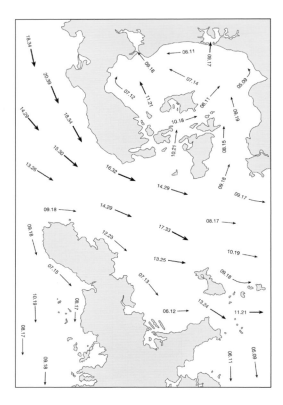

What Causes Tidal Movement?

The gravitational pull of the Moon, the Sun and the rotation of the Earth cause tidal movement. This gives two periods of high and two of low water each 24-hour period.

There are approximately twelve hours between each high water and six hours between high and low water.

There are actually 24 hours and 50 minutes between daily tides, hence the reason for high and low water becoming later each day!

Tides are also affected by monthly variations, due to changes in the strength in the gravitational pull. These differences are known as springs and neaps.

Spring and Neap Tides

The amount of tidal rise and fall is dependent on the time of month. Every two weeks, at a full and a new moon, the sun and moon are aligned and therefore boost the gravitational pull. This produces the largest tidal range (a spring tide) and, therefore, the greatest movement of water, resulting in higher high tides and lower low tides. A smaller tidal range can be seen between a new and full moon – a neap tide, which means lower high tides and higher low tides.

This is explained most easily by looking at a tide timetable, where you will see the difference each day in tidal heights over a two-week period.

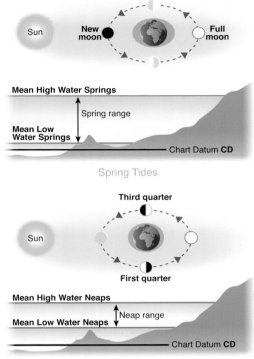

Spring Tides

Neap Tides

Wind and Tide Awareness

Wind Strength – Spotting Gusts and Lulls

It is vital when sailing to be constantly aware of variations in the wind.

- Gusts – increase in wind speed
- Lulls – decrease in wind speed

As you sail along you can spot the following effects.

Differing strengths of wind make fish scales or dark patches (ripples) on the surface. Smooth or calmer water generally indicates lower wind speed, a temporary lull. As the wind freshens, or during a gust, the density of such effects increases, causing the water to become disturbed or choppy, possibly leading to the formation of small waves.

If you sail closely behind or downwind of another sailor, you will be affected by the water state and wind turbulence from their boat.

Gauging the wind strength is a skill that you'll gradually develop. Hand-held wind-speed readers (anemometers) can be useful as a guide to wind strength.

What's under the Water?

The gradient of the beach will determine what the sea state is at different tide levels. This is why it is always a good idea to have a look at a new location at different states of tide and ask others for advice so you can gain more knowledge.

Water Depth

Tides flow faster in deeper channels than in shallow water. For example, in an estuary, where the water is likely to be deeper in the middle, the tidal flow will be greater in the middle than it will be by the shore.

Land Mass

An increase of water flow occurs when tidal streams meet and/or are disrupted by an island, headland or submerged object. This can lead to unusual tidal patterns and water states and may make your sailing unnecessarily challenging. Again, local knowledge can help you identify where such hazards are and how best to deal with them or avoid them altogether.

Wind against Tide

Wind blowing against tidal flow can produce choppy or even very rough conditions, especially if the tidal flow is strong. This may be ideal for the experts, but it's not so good for the intermediate looking for a smooth ride!

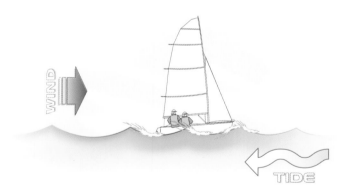

An Upwind Escalator

The tide will take you towards the wind, effectively increasing the wind speed. Especially useful on marginal days, it allows you to practise safe in the knowledge that you are not going to end up miles downwind!

Wind with Tide

Wind blowing with the tide effectively decreases the wind speed. It also produces flatter water but with the added risk that you do have to keep sailing upwind to maintain your position.

Transits

A simple transit is a line between your position on the water and a static visual reference point either on the water (moored boats or buoys) or ashore (building). If the landscape behind this line appears to be stationary (1) then you are not being affected by the tidal stream. If the landscape appears to be moving to the right (starboard (2)) or the left (port (3)) of the transit then you are being moved along by the tide, possibly away from your original launching position and sailing line across the wind.

✓ In line and on course (1)

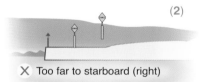

✗ Too far to starboard (right) (2)

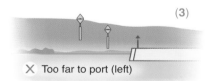

✗ Too far to port (left) (3)

If you choose to sail when the wind and tide are flowing in the same direction, keeping a transit is essential to ensure that you are not drifting too far downwind and down tide. Using the place from which you launched can be the perfect transit and goal point, so remember to glance back several times as you sail away from the shore and take note of what your launch site looks like from the water.

Sailing in Tides

When you sail in coastal waters you need to take the effect of the tide into account. Find out the tide's direction before you go afloat and remember that it is likely to change in strength and direction while you are sailing. If possible, plan to have the tide with you when you head for home to make the return journey easier and to allow for deterioration in the weather.

Conditions will be rougher than usual for the strength of the wind if the wind blows against a strong tidal stream.

TOP TIP

To sail a straight course across a tidal stream or current, line up two fixed objects ahead of you on the shore and keep them in line.

18. STARTING TO RACE

One of the best ways to develop your new-found sailing skills is to start racing. Most clubs organise racing for their members and visitors. Many dinghy, keelboat and multihull classes organise open meetings where you can race against some of the top sailors in your class.

To start with, visit your local sailing club and find someone who needs a crew or, if you have your own boat, join a club that offers racing for the class.

To find your nearest RYA Training Centre visit www.rya.org.uk.

Types of Race Courses

Many different courses can be set to suit the type of boats and local conditions. Dinghies, multihulls and small keelboats often sail a sausage course, featuring a series of upwind and downwind legs, but there are also triangular or square courses. Details of the course will be found in the sailing instructions, together with information on starting signals, special rules etc.

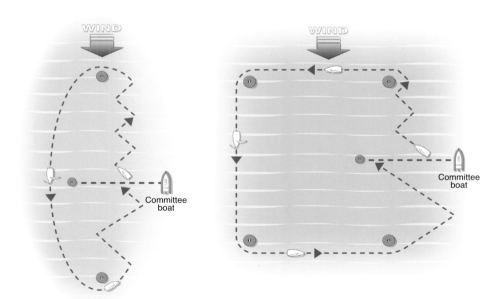

Starting Procedures

The start line will usually be laid at right angles to the wind, often between a committee boat and a small buoy. The race officer will display flags or coloured boards and make sound signals to indicate the course and the countdown to the start. Unless the sailing instructions specify otherwise there will be a warning signal five minutes before the start, followed by a preparatory signal at four minutes to go, a one-minute signal, and the starting signal.

Sailing the Course

For your first few races don't worry if you are left behind by the rest of the fleet – it will take you a little while to understand how to start on time and how to sail at maximum speed. The start and the first leg are of crucial importance. If you get round the first mark near the front of the fleet it will be easier to stay in touch throughout the race.

Practise sailing up to an improvised start line until you can hit the line at full speed on the starting signal. The first leg of the course is nearly always set to windward. It is here that your skill at sailing close-hauled will be tested. If you find that you are sailing slowly compared to other boats around you, look at how they have their sails set and the way they sail their boats and try to copy them.

TOP TIP

Take the RYA Start Racing course and join a club that races dinghies, keelboats or multihulls and get some experience crewing for others before you buy your own boat.

19. WHAT'S NEXT?

RYA Courses

Each RYA National Sailing Scheme course can be taken in dinghies, small keelboats, or multihulls. The initial courses of the Adult (levels 1 and 2) and Youth (stages 1 to 4) sailing schemes will introduce you to this wonderful sport, teaching you all you need to know to get afloat and setting the foundations of sailing.

Having completed the initial courses within the appropriate RYA scheme, in light winds you will be able to rig, launch your boat, sail in all directions, and recover ashore.

Why stop there? Both the Adult and Youth schemes have further courses to assist your progression and increase your confidence in a boat.

Better Sailing (Level 3 in the Adult scheme) progresses skills and techniques, increasing confidence afloat and getting you ready to embark on the Advanced modules.

Following on from the earlier courses, Start Racing and the Advanced modules are designed to suit individual sailing interests. Available both to adults and youth, there are a range of courses to choose from: Seamanship Skills; Day Sailing; Sailing with Spinnakers; and Performance Sailing.

For further details on course content, length, and where your nearest RYA Recognised Training Centre or club is, visit the RYA website www.rya.org.uk.

GLOSSARY

Across the wind	To sail at 90° to the wind. Also known as a beam reach
Aft mainsheet	The mainsheet positioned and laid out at the aft end of the boat
Backed	A sail filled in reverse to the normal direction of the wind. The jib 'backs' to help pull the bow round when tacking
Beam reach	Across the wind – a direction approximately 90° away from the direction of the wind
Bearing away	Turning away from the wind
Boat balance	How flat the boat is, using the crew and helm's weight. One of the Five Essentials
Boat trim	Fore and aft adjustment of the crew's weight to keep the boat level. One of the Five Essentials
Bow	The front of the boat
Broad reach	Direction approximately 135° away from the direction of the wind
Centre mainsheet	The mainsheet positioned and laid out centrally on a boat
Centreboard	Main foil or hinged plate used to resist sideways movement, or leeway
Centreboard position	Adjustment of the centreboard according to the point of sailing
Close reach	An upwind angle between close-hauled and a beam reach
Close-hauled	Direction approximately 45° away from the direction of the wind
Course	Route being taken to your goal or destination
Crew	The person at the front of the boat, forward of the helm, in a two-person boat
Cross-shore	When the wind direction blows directly across the shore or land

Daggerboard	Main foil or plate used to resist sideways movement or leeway, inserted vertically and not hinged (see Centreboard)
Downwind	A position further away from the wind than you are, or to travel away from the wind on a downwind course
Ebbing	The movement of the tide when it is falling, or going out
Fenders	A bumper used to cushion the movement against another boat or vessel when berthing against a jetty, pontoon or mooring
Flooding	The movement of the tide when it is rising, or coming in
Gybe-oh	The call given by the helm to warn the crew they are initiating the gybe
Gybing	To turn the boat onto a new tack, with the wind behind, taking the stern through the wind
Halyard	Rope or wire used to raise sails and to tension the leading edge
Heel	The leaning of a boat from side to side, windward to leeward
Helm	The person who steers the boat, sat to the rear
High pressure	A weather system, also known as an 'anticyclone' or 'high'
Hoisting	Attaching and raising the sails
In irons	When a boat stops head to wind unintentionally, losing rudder effect
Inversion	When a boat capsizes and turns completely upside down
Jib	The smaller sail on a boat, which is in front of the mast
Jib sheet	The rope used to control the angle of the jib
Kicking strap	A rope or wire used to pull down the boom. Also known as a 'kicker' or 'vang'. Important for controlling twist in the mainsail
Lee shore	'Onshore' – when the wind blows in a direction onto the shore

Leech	Back edge or trailing edge of the sail
Lee-oh	The call given by the helm to warn the crew they are initiating the tack
Leeward	The downwind side of the boat, or the direction the wind is blowing to
Low pressure	A weather system, also known as a 'depression' or 'low'
Luff	a) To turn the boat towards the wind b) The term used for the leading edge of a sail
Lying-to	A manoeuvre to stop the boat temporarily by turning it onto a close reach and letting the sails out until they flap on the leeward side
Mainsail	The key sail, behind the mast, on a boat. If a boat only has one sail it has a mainsail
Mainsheet	The rope used to control the angle of the mainsail
Moorings	A temporary or permanent berth for a craft
Multihull	A boat with two parallel hulls. Also called a catamaran
Point of sailing	A boat's position in relation to the wind
Pontoon	A floating platform to stop at or provide a permanent home for a craft
Port	Left
Port tack	Sailing with the wind on the port side
Ready about	A call given by the helm to warn the crew to get ready to tack
Reefing	To reduce the amount of sail used
Rigging	The procedure for attaching and hoisting the sails
Rudder	Flat blade attached to the boat's transom, assisting the steering of the boat

Run	Sailing downwind, approximately 180° away from the direction of the wind
Sail trim	Setting the sails properly in relation to the course being sailed
Sheets	The ropes which control the sails
Shrouds	Side wires which hold up the mast
Springs	Ropes used and positioned to stop the boat moving fore and aft when moored
Stand by to gybe	The call given by the helm to warn the crew to get ready to gybe
Starboard	Right
Starboard tack	Sailing with the wind on the starboard side
Stern	The back of the boat
Tacking	To turn the boat onto a new tack, on an upwind course, taking the boat's bow through the wind
Tell-tales	Wool or lightweight tape used to detect airflow
Tiller extension	Attached to the end of the tiller, which is used to steer the rudder
Toestraps	Used when hiking to stop you falling out, and help keep the boat flat
Training run	A more stable course downwind than a run, a position upwind from a run where the jib just fills
Transit	Two fixed objects in line
Windward	The side of the boat which is closest to the wind, with the wind blowing onto it, i.e. the upwind side. Also used as 'windward boat' – the boat closest to the wind
Windward shore	'Offshore' – when the wind blows in a direction away from the shore. Also called a weather shore

WHY JOIN THE RYA?

OVER 80

RYA member reward partners

Influencing policy on over 250 marine protected areas in UK waters

Fighting for members' rights on more than 20 Current Affairs topics

OnBoard has introduced over

800,000

children to sailing

60,000+

disabled people have been able to experience sailing through the RYA Sailability programme

2,500 international training centres including the UK, Australia, New Zealand, South Africa, Indonesia, Thailand and the USA

250,000

course completions each year

Membership costs from only

12p per day

OVER 815,000

visits to our Knowledge and Advice web pages a year